FARM ANIMALS
Drawing in Color

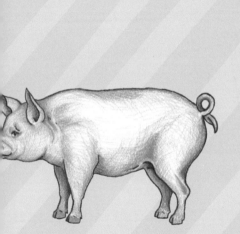

Table of Contents

Are you ready for Drawing In Color?

This book will teach you a simple step-by-step process of drawing. You will see how all images can be broken down into basic shapes. These shapes create the underlying form for the image. Once the form is developed, details like texture and expression lines are added to make the image more realistic.

When you are ready, continue to improve your drawing skills by sketching and coloring the illustrations and photographs included in the back of this book. Use the drawing grids to keep everything in correct proportion.

With these clear step-by-step instructions, you will learn how easy it is to draw any image you want!

Drawing begins with very simple shapes: geometric shapes and organic shapes. Geometric shapes such as the square, circle, and triangle, are known around the world so everyone can use them as a guide for drawing. They have uniform measurements and their shapes are not usually seen in nature. Organic shapes are fluid, loose, and found in nature: rocks, clouds, and leaves, for example.

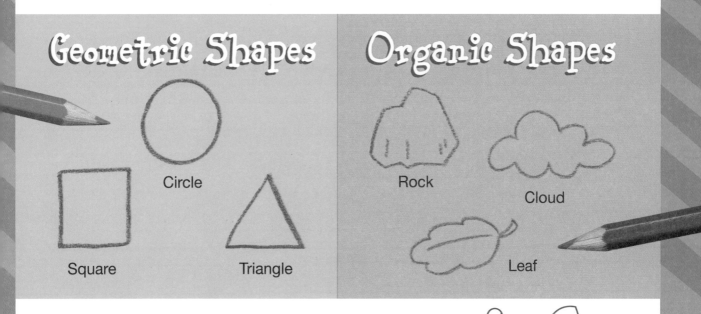

Geometric Shapes

Circle

Square

Triangle

Organic Shapes

Rock

Cloud

Leaf

With each of the animal drawings in this book, you will begin by drawing geometric shapes to create the basic figure. Then you will draw organic shapes to make the figure more natural. Next, you will develop texture and details by adding more organic shapes and lines. When you draw the details of the animal's face, remember that you are developing its emotional expression. Little changes in the eyes, nose, and mouth will bring a unique feeling to each drawing you create.

The Grid System

The step-by-step instructions include a visual aid tool called a grid, which is made up of either 9 or 12 squares. The grid is a guide that will help you draw correct proportions, which is the relationship between the size and location of the different parts of the animal.

In addition, four instruction grids are shown for each animal drawing. The first grid indicates where to place the basic geometric shapes. Grids for steps 2, 3 and 4 show the organic shapes, texture and details. The red lines in grids 1, 2, and 3 show the new lines you will draw in that step.

As you draw, look back and forth between the instruction grids and your drawing grid to see where the drawing lines meet or cross the grid lines. Try to focus on drawing one square at a time. The size and location of your lines will result in a realistically proportioned animal if you follow the proportions of the grid guide drawing. Changing proportions distorts or exaggerates features, which some artists do on purpose.

Now, let's learn drawing made easy!

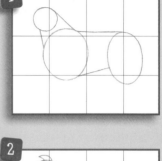

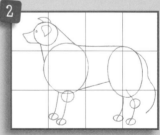

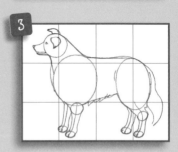

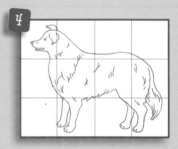

Coloring with Pencils

Add color to your drawing by starting out lightly and working up to darker shades.

Pressing down lightly   Pressing down hard

Build depth and texture into your sketches by blending and layering your colors for a painterly feel.

Here is the full spectrum of colors:

Dark Blue   Light Blue   Green   Yellow   Orange   Red   Violet

Medium Blue   Blue Green   Yellow Green   Yellow Orange   Red Orange   Red Violet

Let the white of the paper show through to bring highlights and light areas to your drawing.

Important Tips:

- You will need to sketch outlines before adding color. Use the drawing pencil included to make all the sketches.

- Before beginning to sketch, practice drawing circles, ovals, and lines on a sheet of paper. This will help you gain better control of your hand.

- Sketch the geometric shapes lightly. You will be drawing over them and erasing them as you finish your sketches.

- Mistakes are a natural and expected part of the drawing process, so keep your eraser handy!

- When adding color to your sketch, start off lightly. Note that colored pencil marks are difficult to erase.

- Keep drawing! The more you draw, the more your drawing skills will improve and your confidence as an artist will grow.

HOW TO DRAW A PIG

Suggested colors:

1 Basic Shapes

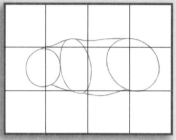

Before you begin, study the size and location of the shapes on the grid so that your proportions are correct. Draw a large oval for the front of the body. Add a circle for the head. Draw two curved lines to connect the head to the front body. A slightly angled circle forms the back hip area. Draw two curved lines connecting the front body to the back hip. The top line is the back; the bottom line is the stomach.

2 More Features

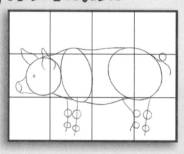

Draw an oval for the snout and two curved lines that connect the snout to the head. Add an eye. To form the ears, draw two wide ovals with pointed tops. Draw a curved line with a loop in it for the tail. Draw two lines for the front legs and two slightly-curved lines for the back legs. Add eight circles for the leg joints.

3 Adding Details

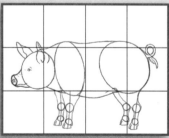

Time to draw organic shapes. Notice how these red lines are mostly curvy. Draw a curved line to form the outer front edge of each ear. Add lines and shapes for the snout, mouth, and eyes. Draw curved lines to finish the width of the legs, hooves, and tail. Add a few extra lines to widen the tip of the tail. Be sure to draw the line indicating the dented area where the back upper leg meets the lower stomach area.

4 Finishing Touches

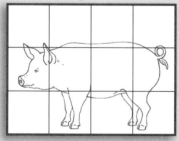

Erase the geometric shapes that remain visible. Now the pig is more lifelike because the organic shapes add form. Draw angled lines to close off the top shape of the hooves. Draw the final details in the face to express your pig's personality. Will your pig's mouth form a slight smile, as in this drawing?

TIP:

Place a sheet of paper under the side of your drawing hand as you sketch. This will keep your hand from smudging the pencil marks as you move along the paper surface.

Did you know?
Pigs have no sweat glands so they roll around in mud to cool down.

HOW TO DRAW A RABBIT

Suggested colors:

1 Basic Shapes

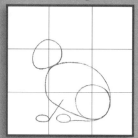

Start by drawing a large oval for the body. Notice the oval's irregular shape that forms the rabbit's chest area. Draw a circle inside the lower back part of the oval to form the hip and upper leg area. Draw an egg-shaped oval for the rabbit's head. Add an angled line for the front leg. Draw a straight horizontal line for the back leg. Draw one oval at the end of each line for the rabbit's feet.

2 More Features

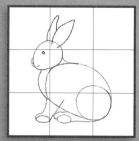

Draw a small circle for the eye. Form the rabbit's nose and mouth by adding two small curves. For the ears, draw two long, narrow oval shapes with pointed tips. Draw a curved line connecting the back of the head to the upper body, forming the neck. Connect the chest to the rabbit's lower chin area with a curved line. Draw two curved lines to complete the width of each leg and foot.

3 Adding Details

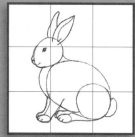

Now, organic shapes. Draw a curved, then short straight line, to form the inside of the rabbit's ear. Add detail to form the eyelid. Draw a curved line to make the area between the eye and the top of the nose a bit higher. Draw a small line indenting where the lower chin meets the upper chest. Add inside leg lines to form four legs. Draw the indents for the toenails. Draw a half-circle with a few choppy lines on top to form the tail.

4 Finishing Touches

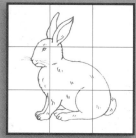

Erase the geometric shapes that are visible. Now the rabbit is more lifelike because the organic shapes add form. To add fur texture, draw many short, slightly curved lines grouped together over several areas of the rabbit's body, legs, and tail. Draw the final details in the face, including the short eyebrows and the long whiskers. Notice there is also a small dent line now near the lower ear edge.

Did you know?
A rabbit's teeth never stop growing.
However, constant gnawing wears
down the teeth and prevents them
from growing too long.

9

HOW TO DRAW A CHICKEN

Suggested colors:

1 Basic Shapes

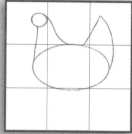

Start by drawing a large oval for the middle of the chicken body. Add a triangle for the shoulders and neck, making a small curve on the triangle's right side, which would be the back of the neck. Draw a small oval over the top point of the triangle for the chicken head. Add a triangle for the back tail, curving the right side to form the area at the back of the tail.

2 More Features

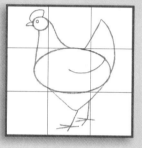

Draw a curved rectangle on top of the oval to form the chicken's comb. Next, draw a small circle for the eye. Draw a slightly curved triangle for the beak and a long curve for the wing. Draw an upside-down triangle for the lower part of the chicken body. One vertical line forms each leg; at the bottom of each, add four lines to form the chicken feet.

3 Adding Details

Time to draw organic shapes. Notice how these red lines are uneven and curvy. They may be close to, or far away from, the geometric shapes. Draw curvy lines in the tail and wing feathers. Draw lines to form the back leg area. Chicken combs and wattles come in many different shapes, so draw an extra bump or two when you draw these areas on your chicken's head. Refine the shape of the beak.

4 Finishing Touches

Erase the geometric shapes that remain visible. Now the chicken is more lifelike because the organic shapes add form. To add texture such as feathers, draw many short, slightly curved lines in the chest, neck, wing, body, and tail areas. Draw the final details in the face. Will your chicken have a large or small eye? Try a small one first; then, if you want it bigger, add to the outside eye shape.

Did you know?

Chickens live together as a flock and will take care of each other's eggs and chicks.

HOW TO DRAW A CAT

Suggested colors:

1 Basic Shapes

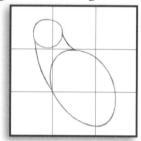

Before you begin drawing, pay attention to where both the oval and the circle shape are on the grid so that your proportions are correct. Start by drawing a large leaning oval for the body. Next, draw a circle for the cat head. Draw two curved lines to connect the head to the body. One line forms the front of the neck and chest. The other line forms the back of the neck.

2 More Features

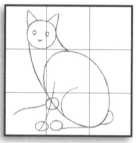

Draw two triangles for ears. Add two circles for eyes; if you want, make yours bigger or smaller. A half-circle with two curved lines on each end forms the nose. Draw a half-circle where the tail connects to the body; add a curvy line where the end of the tail comes out in front of the cat. A curve forms the bottom back leg/knee area. Draw a line for the front leg and back leg and a circle for each cat paw.

3 Adding Details

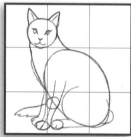

Time to draw organic shapes. Notice how these red lines are uneven and curvy. They may be close to, or far away from, the geometric shapes. Add some extra width to the ears and add a line for the inner front of each ear. Draw the eyelids at an angle and draw two curves to form the mouth. Add some width around the cat's body. Draw lines to form the tail and leg shapes.

4 Finishing Touches

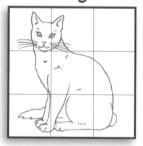

Erase the geometric shapes that remain visible. Now the cat is more lifelike because the organic shapes add form. To add fur texture, draw many short lines in the outline of the inner ears, outer cheeks, chest, stomach, body, leg, and tail areas. Add detail to the cat paws. Draw the final details in the face. Add line shapes to the cat eyelids and pupils. Add whiskers: long or short, many or few!

13

HOW TO DRAW A COW

Suggested colors:

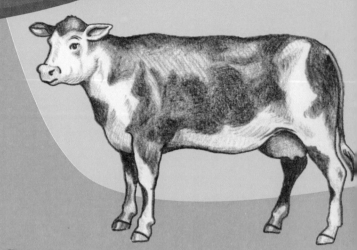

1 Basic Shapes

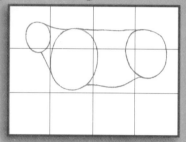

Before you begin, study the size and location of the shapes on the grid so that your proportions are correct. Draw a large circle for the front of the body. Add an egg shape for the head. Draw two curved lines to connect the head to the front body. Add an oval for the back hip area. Draw two lines connecting the front body to the back hip oval. The top line is the back; the bottom line is the stomach.

2 More Features

To form the muzzle, draw a half-circle with a bump. Add an eye. To form the ears, draw two sideways ovals with pointed tops. Draw a curvy line for the tail. Next, add two lines for the front legs. Draw two slightly curved lines for the back legs. Draw eight circles for the leg and ankle joints. A circle forms the cow's udder area.

3 Adding Details

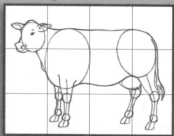

Time to draw organic shapes: the uneven and curvy red lines. Add curved lines for the nose and mouth. Add details to the eye area. Draw lines to indicate the front edge of the ears. Add a curve for the upper back shape. Draw lines to finish the width of the legs, hooves, and tail. Draw in the two bumps to the udder outline. Add lines to make the tail tip fuller.

4 Finishing Touches

Erase the geometric shapes that remain visible. Now the cow looks more lifelike because the organic shapes add form. Draw angled lines to close off the top shape of the hooves. Draw the final details in the face and mouth to express your cow's personality. Draw small lines on the body to show where bones and muscle create hills and valleys in the cow's shape.

Use the side of your pencil to create soft, grainy shading. The tip of your pencil will allow you to add denser coloring to your sketch.

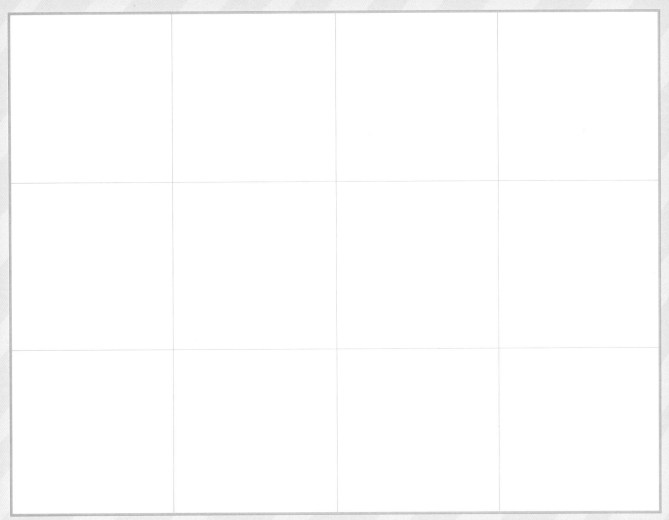

Did you know?

A group of 12 or more cows is called a flink.

HOW TO DRAW A SHEEP

Suggested colors:

1 Basic Shapes

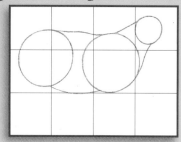

Before you begin, study the size and location of the shapes on the grid so that your proportions are correct. Start with a large circle for the front of the body. Draw a circle for the head. Add two curved lines to connect the head to the front body. Draw a circle for the back hip area. Draw two curved lines connecting the front body to the back hip. The top line is the back; the bottom line is the stomach.

2 More Features

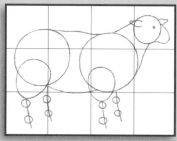

Draw a half-oval for the muzzle. Add an eye. To form the ears, draw two sideways ovals with pointed tops. Draw two egg shapes for the area at the top of the sheep's legs. Create the front legs by adding two lines. Draw two lines for the back legs. Add eight circles for the leg joints.

3 Adding Details

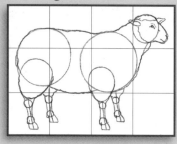

Time to draw organic shapes. Form the front inside of each ear with curved lines. Draw curves to form the wool cap on top of the head, the jawline, and the upper neck area. Add curves for the nose, lips, chin, and eyes. Draw lines for the upper legs and to finish the width of the lower legs and hooves. Draw short bumpy lines along the outlines to show lumpy wool all over the sheep.

4 Finishing Touches

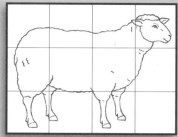

Erase the geometric shapes that remain visible. Now the sheep is more lifelike because the organic shapes add form. Draw angled lines to close off the top shape of the hooves. Draw the final details in the face to express your sheep's personality. Draw more bumpy and curved lines throughout the sheep's body, chest, neck, and upper legs to show the lumpy areas of wool.

IDEA:

Create a scrapbook of inspiration. Collect newspaper and magazine clippings as well as old postcards and photos.

Did you know?

An adult sheep is sheared once a year for its wool The wool from one sheep is called a fleece.

HOW TO DRAW A GOOSE

Suggested colors:

1 Basic Shapes

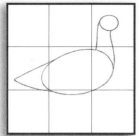

Start by drawing a large oval for the middle of the goose body. Draw a small oval up above for the goose head. Add two curved lines to connect the head to the body; the lines should have long curves to form the neck and front chest areas. Add a curved triangle for the back tail, curving the lower edge more to form a wider sloping area on the bottom of the tail.

2 More Features

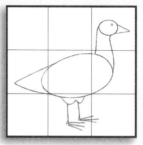

Draw a small circle for the eye. Form the beak with a slightly curved triangle. Draw the lower part of the goose body above the leg. Draw one vertical line for each leg; at the bottom of each leg, add three lines to form the goose's feet.

3 Adding Details

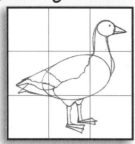

Time to draw organic shapes. Notice how these red lines are uneven and curvy. Draw several curvy lines to form the body, the wings, and the tail feathers. Note the hard upwards turn in the line that forms the wing shape in the goose's shoulder area. Refine the shape of the lines forming the mouth in the beak. Draw lines to complete the width of the legs and webbed feet.

4 Finishing Touches

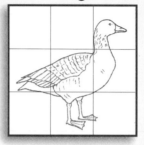

Erase any visibly remaining geometric shapes. Now the goose is much more lifelike. To add feather texture, draw many short, slightly curved lines in the neck and wing areas. Draw the final details in the face. Will your goose have a large or small eyelid? Add details to the upper beak area for the nose. Add details to the webbed feet so you can see where the long toes meet the webbing.

TIP:
Use your eraser to lighten areas in your sketch.

Did you know?

A female duck is called a hen.
A male duck is called a drake.

HOW TO DRAW A GOAT

Suggested colors: ●●●●●●

1 Basic Shapes

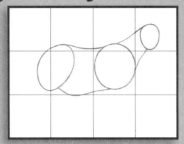

Before you begin, study the size and location of the shapes on the grid so that your proportions are correct. Draw a large circle for the front of the body. Continue with a circle for the head. Add two curved lines to connect the head to the front body. Draw an oval for the back hip area. Add two lines connecting the front body to the back hip oval. The top line is the back; the bottom line is the stomach.

2 More Features

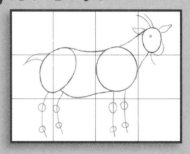

Start adding features by adding a half-circle for the muzzle. Next, add an eye. To form the ears, draw two ovals with pointed tops. Draw two curves for the horns and add a line for the goat's beard. A curved triangle forms the tail. Draw two lines for the front legs and two slightly curved lines for the back legs. Draw eight circles for the leg joints.

3 Adding Details

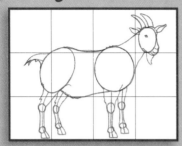

Time to draw organic shapes. Notice how these red lines are uneven and curvy. They may be close to, or far away from, the geometric shapes. Draw a curved line to form the front inside of each ear. Add curved lines for the nose, mouth, and chin. Draw curves to finish the width of the horns, beard, legs, hooves, and tail. Add short choppy lines to the tail, stomach, shoulder, and upper legs to show fur.

4 Finishing Touches

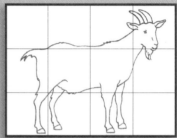

Erase the geometric shapes that remain visible. Now the goat is more lifelike because the organic shapes add form. To finish the beard, add curvy lines. Draw angled lines to close off the top shape of the hooves. Draw the final details in the face to express your goat's personality.

TIP:

Blend different colored pencils together to create depth and texture in your sketch.

Did you know?

Both male and female goats have beards.

HOW TO DRAW A DONKEY

Suggested colors:

1 Basic Shapes

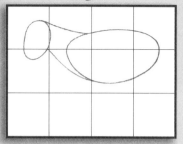

Before you begin, study the size and location of the shapes on the grid so that your proportions are correct. Start with a very large oval for the body. Draw an egg shape for the head, with the narrow part placed where the mouth will be drawn. Draw two curved lines to connect the head to the body. The top line is the back of the neck; the bottom line is the front of the neck.

2 More Features

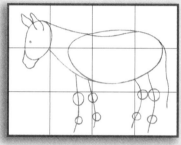

Draw a half-circle for the muzzle. Add an eye. To form the ears, draw two ovals, extending their ends into pointed tops. Draw a curved line to show where the donkey's spine dips along its back. A curvy line forms the tail. Draw one line for the front leg and an angled line for the back front leg. Draw two slightly curved lines for the back legs. Add eight circles for the leg and ankle joints.

3 Adding Details

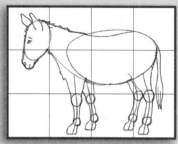

Time to draw organic shapes: the uneven and curvy red lines. Draw short, choppy lines for the short mane lying on the forehead and neck. Add curved lines for the nose and mouth. Detail the shapes in the eye area. Draw lines to finish the width of the legs, hooves, and tail. Add short lines to the outline for hair on the front neck and chest areas. Draw lines to make the tail tip fuller.

4 Finishing Touches

Erase the geometric shapes that remain visible. Now the donkey looks more lifelike because the organic shapes add form. Draw angled lines to close off the top shape of the hooves. Draw the final details in the face to express your donkey's personality. Draw small lines on the face and body to show where bones and muscle create detail in the donkey's shape.

TIP:
Notice each animal has white highlights in its eyes. When drawing eyes, be sure to make a small circle for the highlight and color in the pupils on the outside.

Did you know?

A donkey's strong sense of self-preservation makes it appear stubborn. Sensing danger, it will not budge.

HOW TO DRAW A DOG

Suggested colors:

1 Basic Shapes

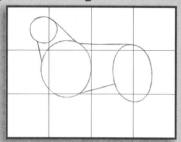

Before you begin, study the size and location of the shapes on the grid so that your proportions are correct. Draw a large circle for the front of the body. Continue by drawing a circle for the head. Draw two curved lines to connect the head to the front body. Next, draw an oval for the back hip and upper leg area. Draw two lines connecting the front body to the oval. The top line is the back; the bottom line is the stomach.

2 More Features

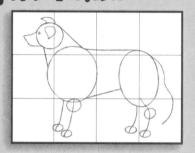

Draw a slightly curved, bulky rectangle for the muzzle. Add an eye. To form the ear, draw a half-circle with a line closing it off. A curvy line forms the tail. Draw two lines for the front legs and two slightly curved lines for the back legs. Add two circles for the leg joints and four circles for the paws.

3 Adding Details

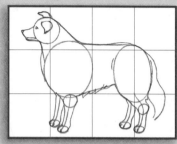

Time to draw organic shapes. Notice how these red lines are uneven and curvy. They may be close to, or far away from, the geometric shapes. Add some extra length to the ear and finish in a point. Add a nose. Draw a line for the mouth. Add lines to complete the width of the tail, four legs, and paws. Add some short choppy lines around the body outline to show fur.

4 Finishing Touches

Erase the geometric shapes that remain visible. Now the dog is more lifelike because the organic shapes add form. To add more fur texture for this heavy-coated dog, draw many short lines throughout all the body parts. Add detail to the paws. Draw the final details in the face. The shape of your dog's ear, eyes, mouth, and tail express personality, alertness, curiosity, and emotions.

IDEA:

Try sketching your own pet from a photograph.
Take the photo at their level for the best angle.

Did you know?

Collies are highly intelligent
and must have tasks to perform.
They are known for their
intense herding instinct.

HOW TO DRAW A ROOSTER

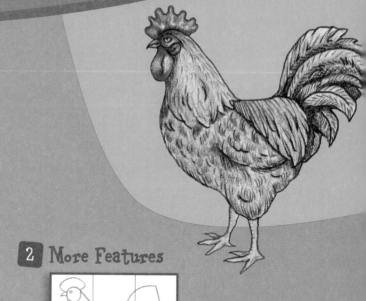

Suggested colors:

1 Basic Shapes

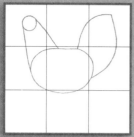

Start by drawing a large oval for the middle of the rooster body. Draw a triangle for the shoulders, chest, and neck, making a slight curve on the triangle's lower left side, which would be the chest area. Draw a small circle over the top point of the triangle for the rooster head. Add two long curved lines to form the back tail.

2 More Features

Draw a curved rectangle on top of the oval to form the comb. Draw a small circle for the eye and a slightly curved triangle for the beak. Next, draw a curve from the triangle front down to the body oval. Draw a long curve for the wing and a half-oval for the upper part of the rooster leg. Draw one vertical line for each leg; at the bottom of each, add four lines to form the rooster feet.

3 Adding Details

Time to draw organic shapes. Notice how these red lines are uneven and curvy. They may be close to, or far away from, the geometric shapes. Draw curvy lines in the tail and wing. A short curve connects the lower body to the back leg area. Draw the front lines for the rooster legs and the lines to finish the feet shapes. Refine the shape of the beak. Draw a unique rooster comb and wattle.

4 Finishing Touches

Erase the geometric shapes that remain visible. Now the rooster is more lifelike because the organic shapes add form. To add texture such as feathers, draw many short, slightly curved lines in the chest, neck, wing, body, and tail areas. Draw the final details in the face. Will your rooster have a large cheek? Try a small one first; then, if you want it bigger, add to the outside cheek shape.

Did you know?

Roosters sit on a high perch to guard flocks of hens from predators.

HOW TO DRAW A HORSE

Suggested colors:

1 Basic Shapes

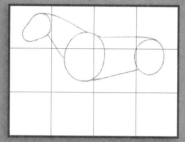

Before you begin, study the size and location of the shapes on the grid so that your proportions are correct. Draw a large circle for the front of the body. Add an egg shape for the head. Draw two curved lines to connect the head to the front body. Then draw an oval for the back hip area. Connect the front body to the back hip oval with two lines. The top line is the back; the bottom line is the stomach.

2 More Features

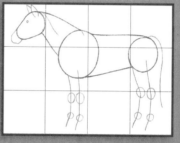

Draw a half-circle for the muzzle. Draw an eye. To form the ears, draw two ovals with pointed tops. Draw a curved line to show where the horse's mane falls along its neck. A curvy line forms the tail. Draw two lines for the front legs and two slightly curved lines for the back legs. Next, add eight circles for the leg and ankle joints.

3 Adding Details

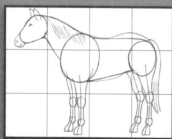

Time to draw organic shapes: the uneven and curvy red lines. They may be close to, or far away from, the geometric shapes. Draw some short lines for the mane lying on the forehead. Add curved lines for the nose and mouth. Extend the shape of the eye. Draw a curve for the upper back hip. Draw lines to finish the width of the legs, hooves and tail. Draw many thin strokes for the mane and tail hair.

4 Finishing Touches

Erase the geometric shapes that remain visible. Now the horse looks more lifelike because the organic shapes add form. Draw angled lines to close off the top shape of the hooves. Add the final details in the face to express your horse's personality. Draw small lines on the face and body to show where bones and muscle create detail in the horse's shape.

IDEA:

When you are more confident in drawing, experiment with different drawing media such as chalk, crayons, pastels and pen and ink.

Did you know?

Horses are traditionally measured in hands. This unit was first defined as the width of a man's hand and has since been set at 4 inches (10 cm).

3

Time to practice drawing in color!

Use the following grid sheets to practice sketching and coloring using the four-step grid system. Try drawing the twelve animals in this book and many more!

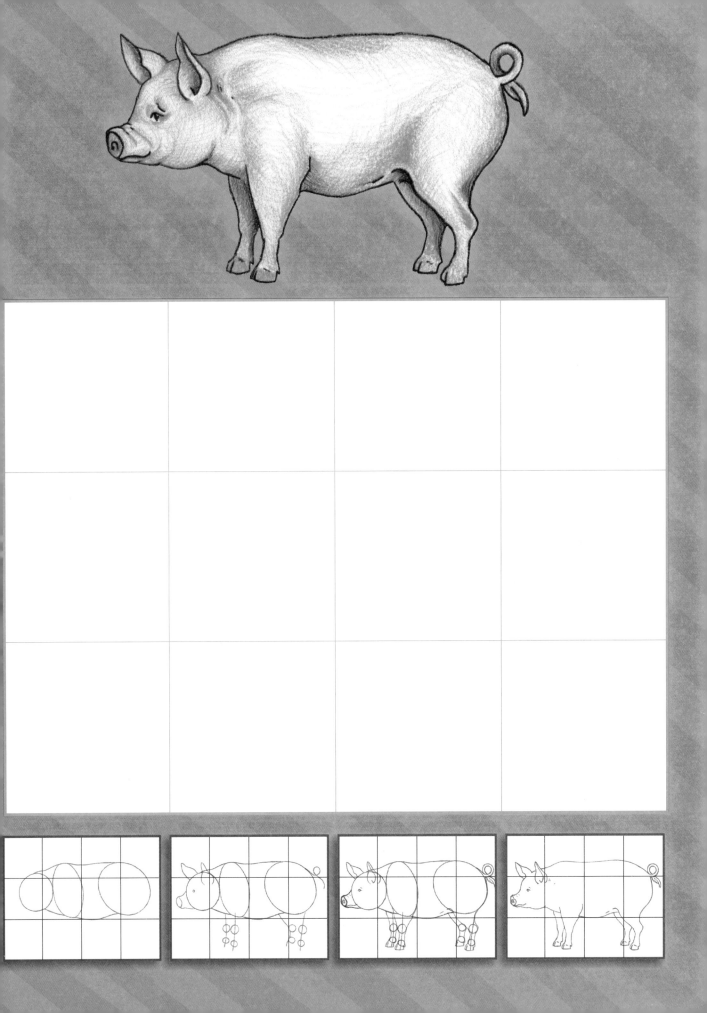

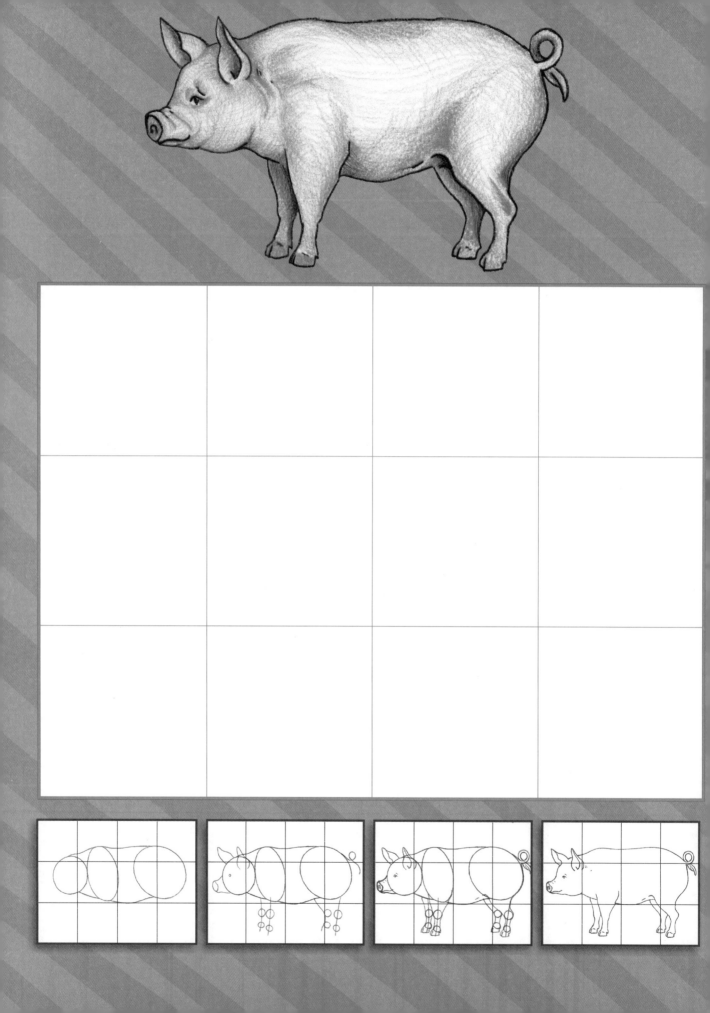

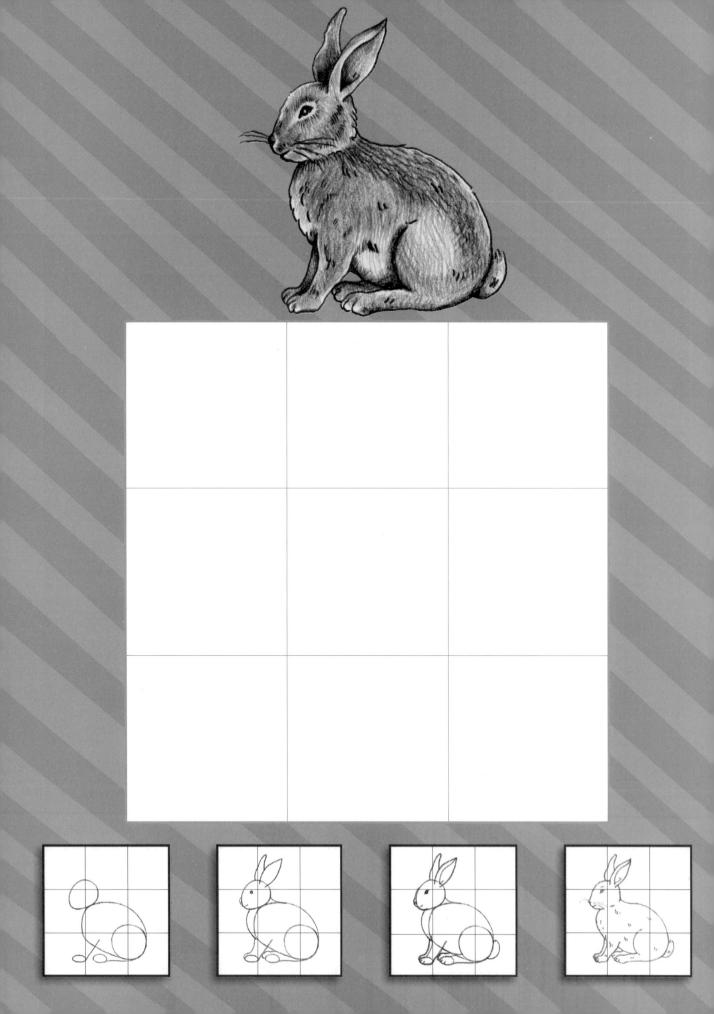

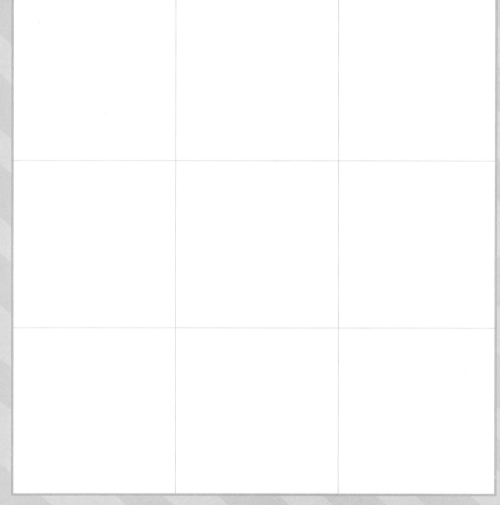

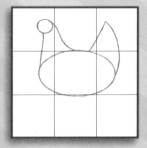

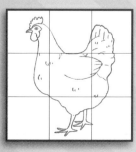

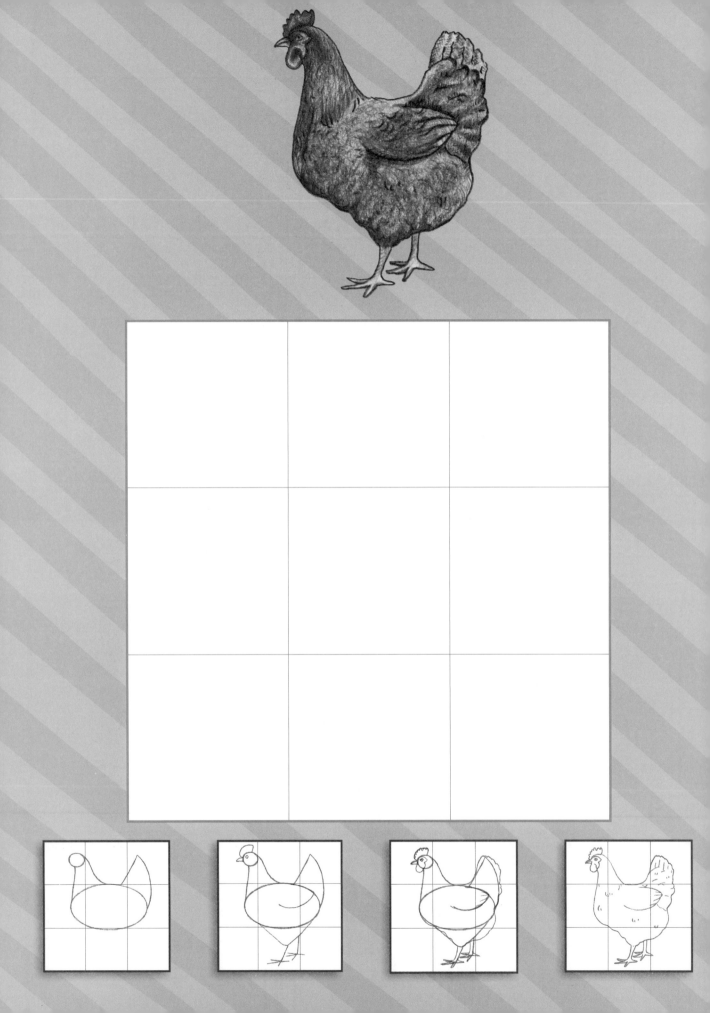

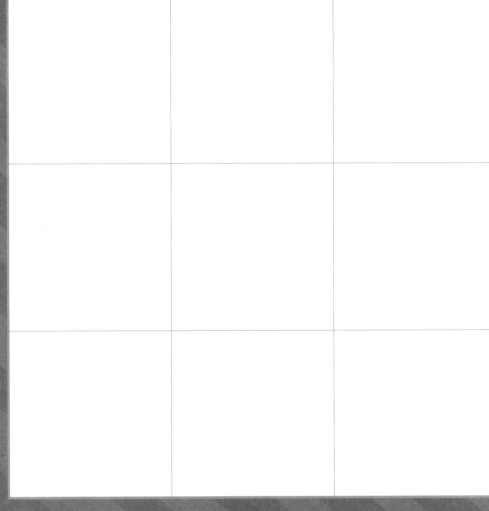

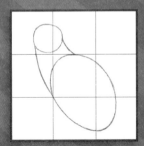

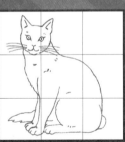

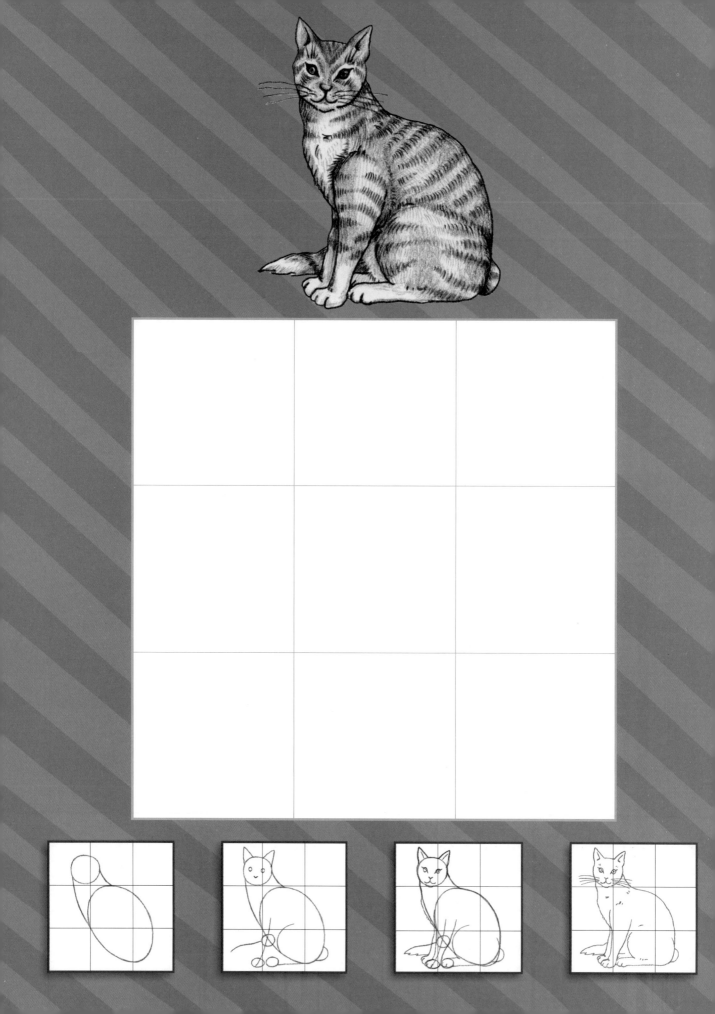

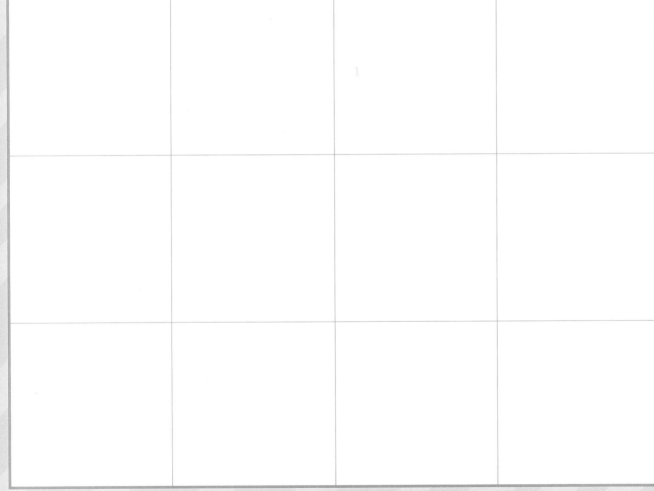

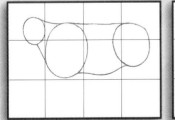
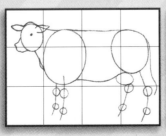
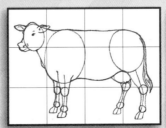
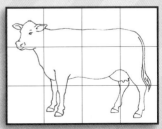

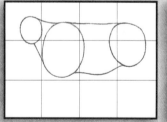 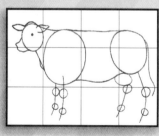 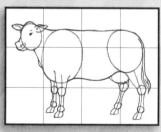 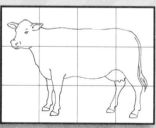

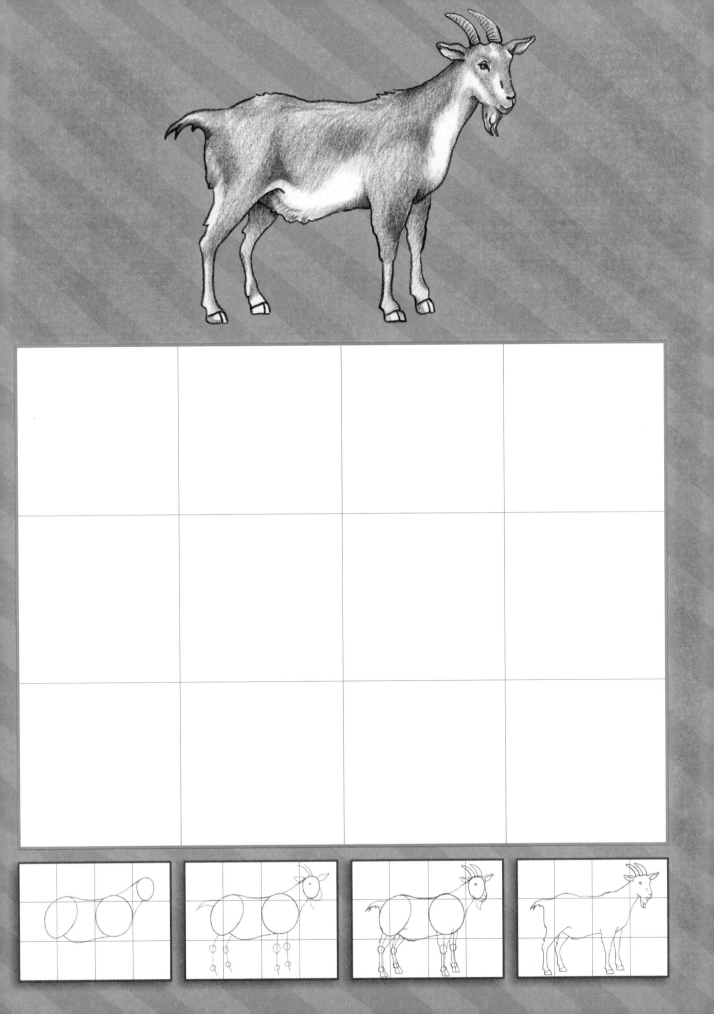

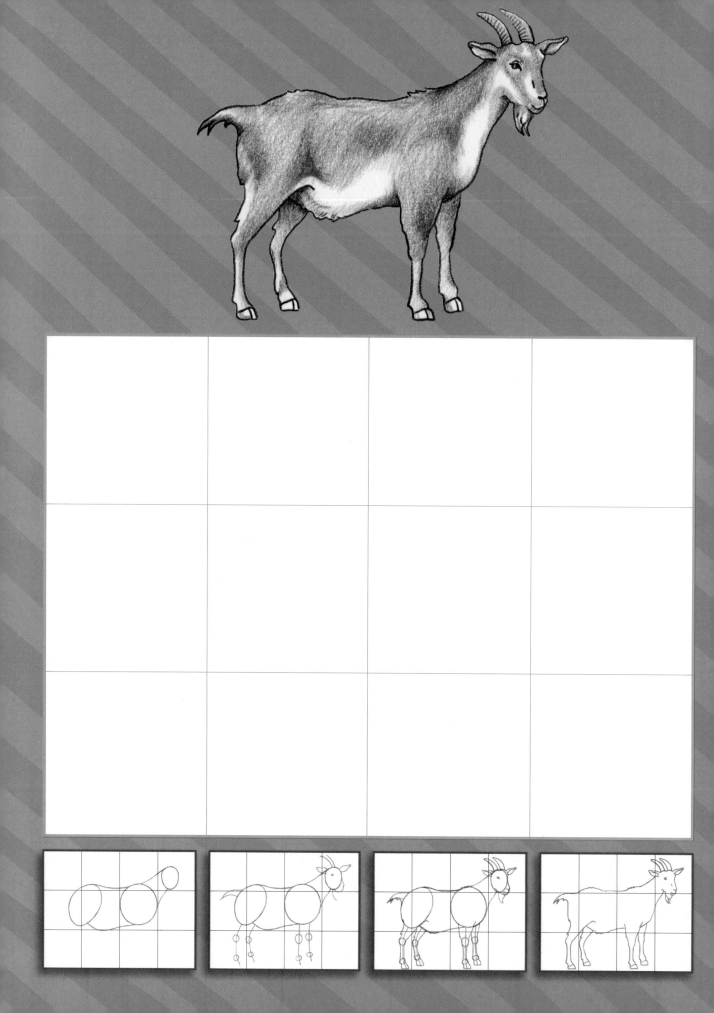

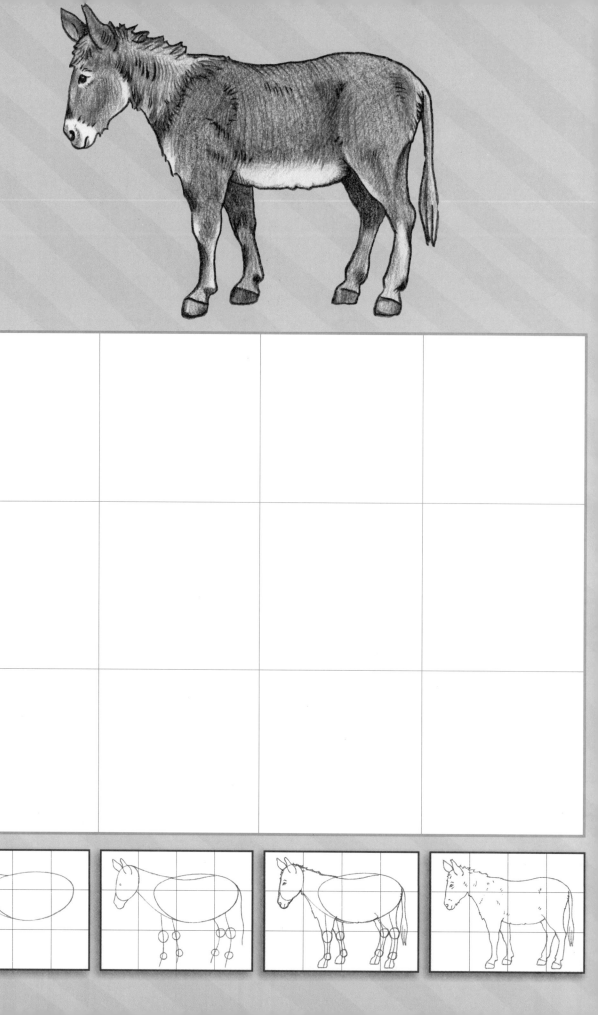

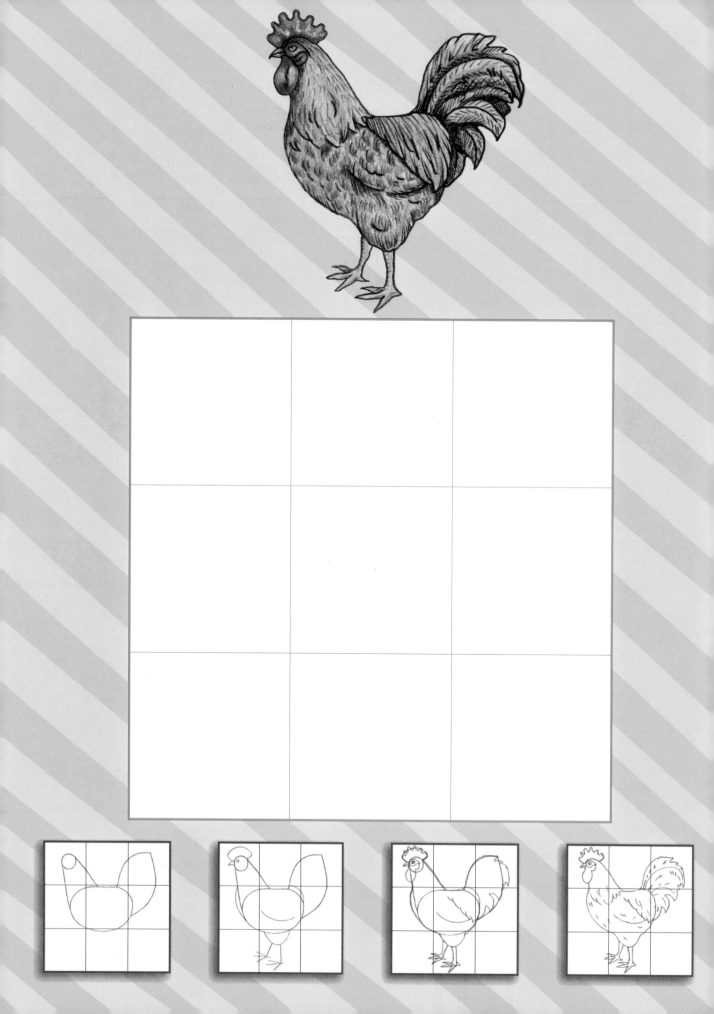

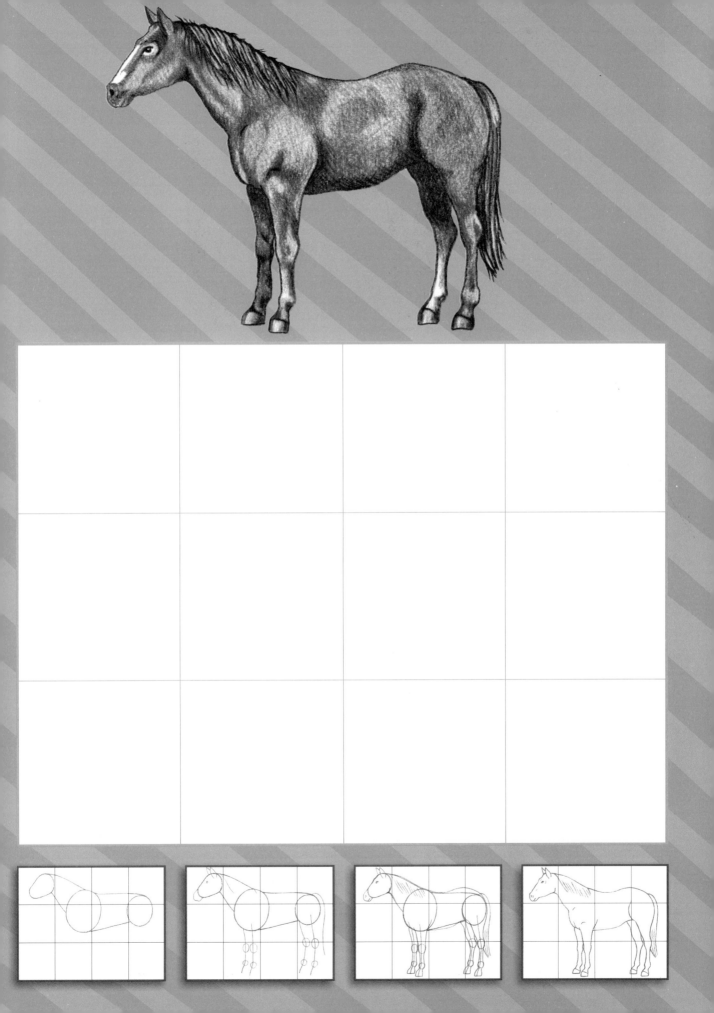

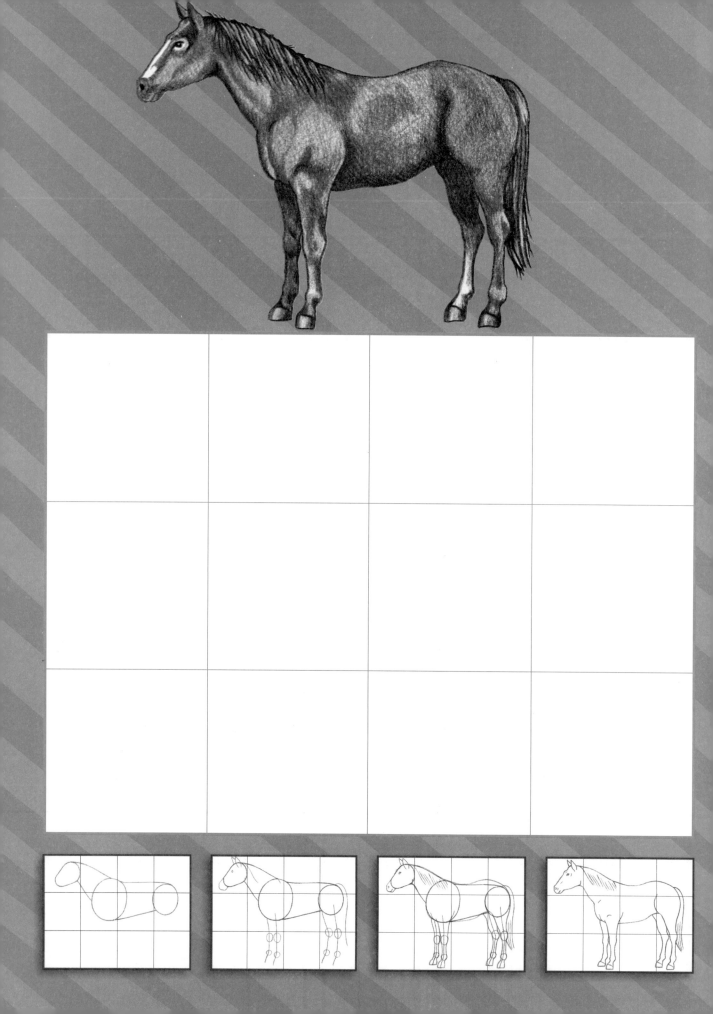

Now that you have learned the simple step-by-step process of drawing with a grid, try to create more realistic sketches from photographs of farm animals.

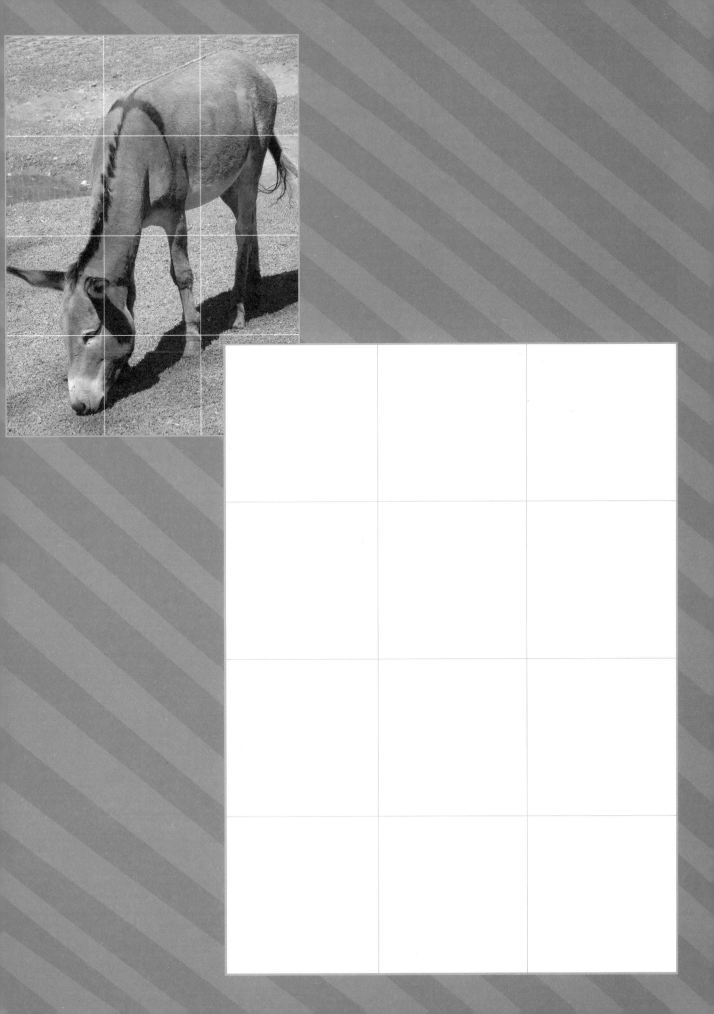

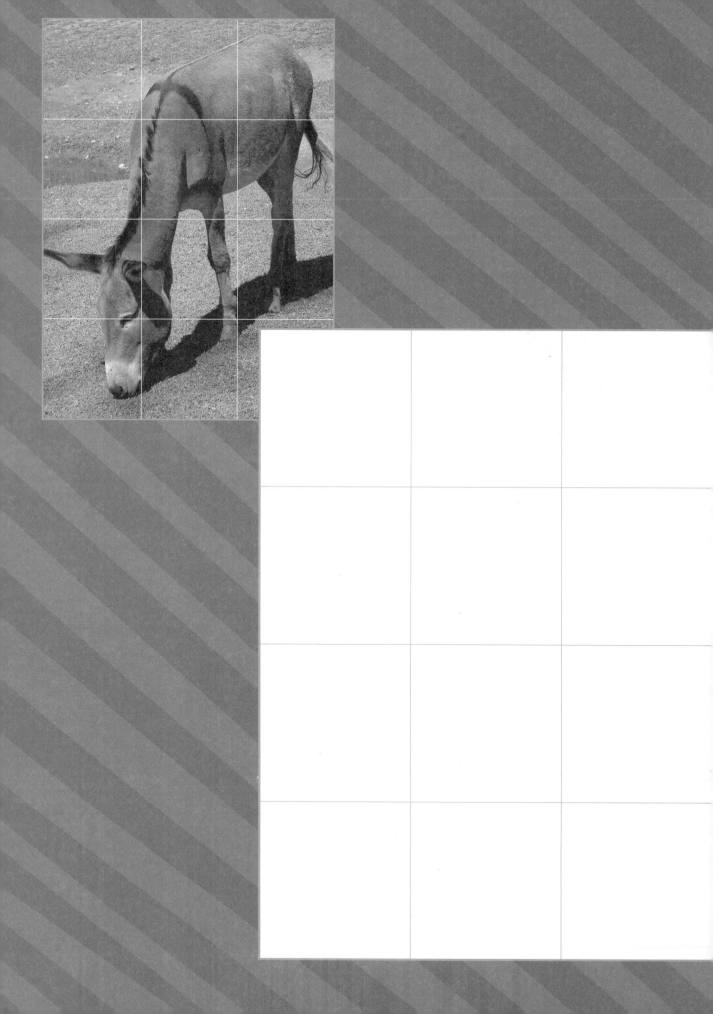

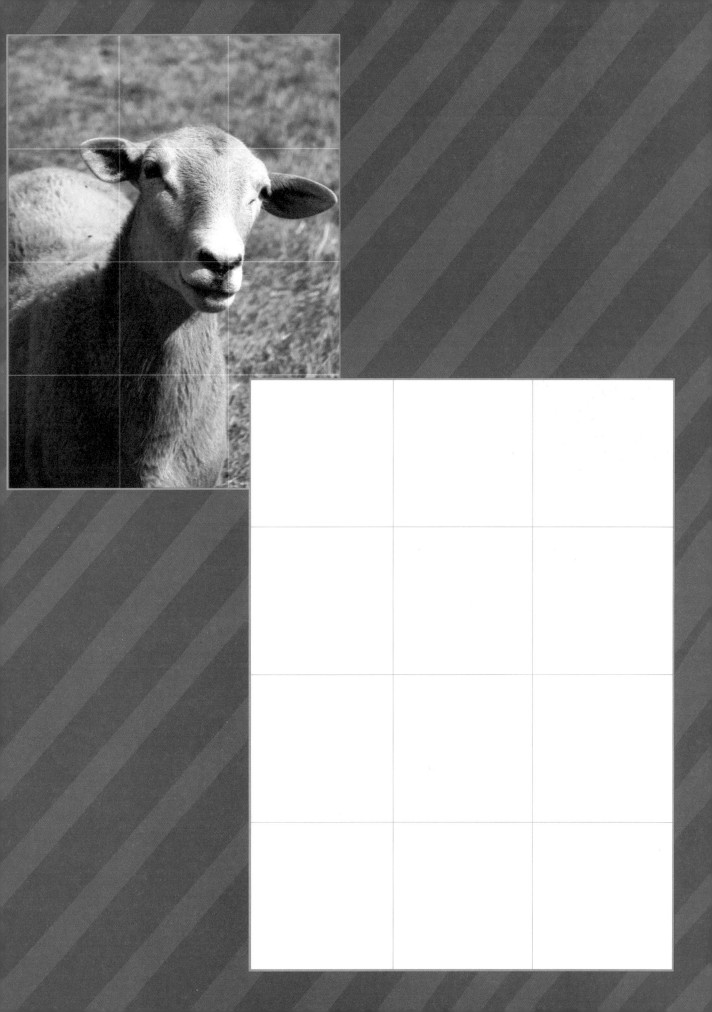

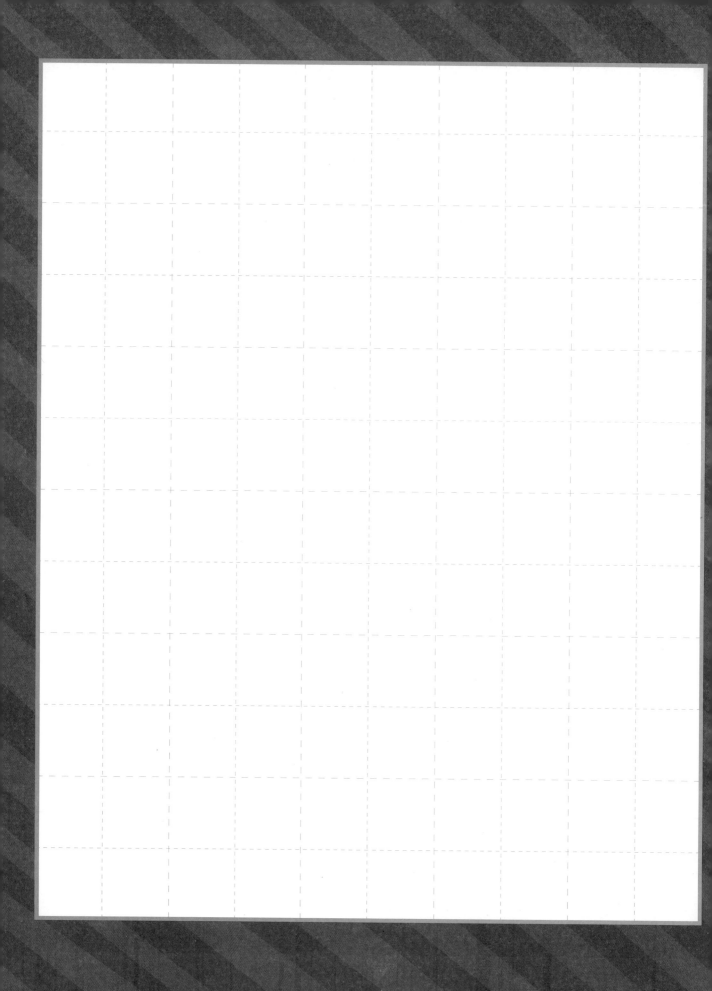